EASY GRAMMAR

A LEARNER-FRIENDLY TEXT

JINCY ISAC

Contents

Contents

Foreword

Prof. K. P. Kuriakose
Associate Professor [Rtd]
St. Peters College, Kolenchery

It is true that there are hundreds of textbooks on English grammar. However, most of them are inaccessible to most of the Indian students who study English. A textbook describing the basic concepts of English grammar within the reach of a common Indian student is the need of the hour. This book has been prepared for meeting this urgent need. The principles of English grammar have been clearly explained here in such a way that every student can follow them without any difficulty. The numerous examples given in every chapter can help the students learn the principles of English grammar easily. This book is undoubtedly learner-friendly and I hope that the book will be well received by those for whom it is written.

Preface

Language is the means by which people communicate and it cannot exist without grammar. If you have a good command of grammar, you have the ability to express yourself well. But nowadays even graduate are unable to speak or write reasonably correct English. I am sure this book will help them to overcome their deficiency. This book has been designed in such a way that the aspirants can learn it by themselves. I hope that this text will be useful for students of all ages.

Acknowledgements

My sincere thanks to **Prof. K. P. Kuriakose** for his suggestions at all stages in the writing of this book.

I owe a deep sense of gratitude to **Mr. Eldhose K. B.** for his kind help and encouragement.

I would like to thank **Prof.Baby M. Varghese, Prof. K. M. Kuriakose**, my venerable teachers, family members and friends for their constant inspiration.

I am extremely grateful to **Dr. Saran S.,** who has undertaken the responsibility of publishing this book.

Author

Jincy Isac
Assistant Professor, Department of English
Yeldo Mar Baselios College, Kothamangalam

Jincy Isac is a passionate teacher with sixteen years of experience in handling English language and grammar classes. She obtained her master's degree from Osmania University, Hyderabad. She started her career as an English teacher at Indira Gandi Arts and science college, Nellikuzhi, Kothamangalam. For the past ten years, she has been working at Yeldo Mar Baselios College, Kothamangalam. Her experience as a teacher who engages in grammar classes for the past 16 years has made her acquainted with the various aspects of grammar and also knows the problems faced by students in the field of grammar. All these varied experiences have made her complete her book on grammar as it is with us now.

Introduction

The English language has the widest reach of any language spoken today.To cope with the modern world, where globalization takes place drastically, acquiring effective skills in English is a must. Besides, the language used must have a degree of correctness in grammar to make it acceptable. Many students have a wrong conception that grammar is a hard nut to crack and they cannot conquer it easily. This text helps the scholar to study grammar without taking the help of any other person as its language is very simple. It covers almost all areas of grammar leading the learners from basics to top-level. Grammar skill seems very important not only in the education sector but also for a smart career. It is an inevitable component in almost all competitive exams at the central and state levels. The simple style of this book makes self-learning easy and even pleasurable.

Parts of Speech

Words are divided into different classes according to the role they play in a sentence. Each class of words is called a part of speech. The parts of speech are eight in number.

1. **Noun**

   A noun is the name of a person, place, animal, or thing. Cat, Raju, Kochi, Pen.

2. **Pronoun**

   A word used instead of a noun is called a pronoun. He, She, It, They

3. **Adjective**

   An adjective is a word that tells something more about a noun.
   Delicious, Brave, Honest.

4. **Verb**

Verbs are words that denote an action, possession, or the state or condition of something.

Roy *killed* the snake.

He *has* two cars.

Veena *is* here to participate in the tournament.

5. **Adverb.**

Adverbs tell us more about verbs. They add meaning to a verb, adjective, or another adverb.

She sang *sweetly*.

These roses are *absolutely* beautiful.

Neha worked *extremely* well.

6. **Preposition.**

Prepositions are words that usually come before a noun or a pronoun in a sentence and show the relationship of a noun or pronoun with other words in the sentence.

In, On, from, over, under, besides.....

The cat is on the box.

The ball is in the box.

7. **Conjunction.**

It is a word used to join words, phrases, or clauses.

And, But, as, well as, though, until, whereas,...

Santhosh *as well as* his friendsare coming to the party.

Though he went early he missed his train.

8. **Interjection.**

It is a word that expresses a sudden emotion.

Wow!, Alas!, Hurry!

Alas! She is sick.

Wow! What a good idea.

Identify the part of speech of each italicized word in the following sentences.

1. I *met* him yesterday.
2. She looks so *beautiful.*
3. He ran *quickly.*
4. He ran fast *but* missed the train.
5. *Alas!* She is not well.

Answers

1. Verb
2. Adjective
3. Adverb
4. Conjunction
5. Interjection

CHAPTER TWO

Subject and Predicate

Every sentence has two parts the subject and the predicate. The part of the sentence which names the person or thing we are speaking about is called the subject.

The part which tells something about the subject is called the predicate. The keyword in the predicate is a verb.

They are playing football.

Here, the subject is 'they 'and the predicate is 'are playing football'.

Separate the subject & predicate in the following sentences.

1. Gopal went to the bank.
2. This flower is very beautiful.
3. The early bird catches the worm.
4. Edison invented the bulb.
5. Australia is the largest island in the world.

Answers

1. Sub: Gopal

    Predicate: went to the bank.
2. Sub: This flower
Predicate: is very beautiful.

2. Sub: The early bird

   Predicate: catches the worm
   4. Sub: Edison
   Predicate: invented the bulb.
   5. Sub: Australia
   Predicate: is the largest island in the world.

CHAPTER THREE

Sentence

A group of words that makes complete sense is called a sentence. A sentence begins with a capital letter and ends with a full stop, question mark, or exclamation mark.

He is a brave boy.

How old are you?

What a Shame!

Phrase

A group of words that makes sense, but not complete sense, is called a phrase.

1) On the notice board.

I saw that picture on the noticeboard

2) With my friends.

I had my dinner with my friends from Taj Restaurant

Types of Sentences

There are four types of sentences.

1.   Assertive / Declarative sentences

A sentence that makes a statement or an assertion is called an assertive sentence. An assertive sentence ends with a full stop.

The Sun rises in the east.

She looks very beautiful.

2. Interrogative sentence

A sentence that asks a question is called an interrogative sentence.

Where is your college?
How old are you?

3. Imperative sentence

A sentence that expresses a command, a request, or a suggestion is called an imperative sentence.

Do your work.
Please give me a pen.
Let's go to the cinema.

4. Exclamatory Sentence

A sentence that expresses a strong feeling or emotion is called an exclamatory sentence.

What lovely music!
Such a beautiful movie!

Identify the four kinds of sentences
1. Can you please close the window.
2. What is your favourite colour?
3. He is the leader of the group
4. How clever she is!
5. This is an interesting novel

Answers
1. Imperative
2. Interrogative
3. Declarative
4. Exclamatory
5. Declarative

CHAPTER FOUR

Noun

We know that the names of people, places, and things are called nouns.

Things that can be counted are **countable nouns**. They can be used in the singular and the plural forms.

Mango – mangoes, table – tables, book – books.

Things that cannot be counted are called **uncountable nouns**. Usually, uncountable nouns do not have plural forms.

Furniture, oil, sand, milk, blood.

Types of Nouns

1. A **proper noun** is the name of a person, place, or thing and it always begins with a capital letter.

    London, Thomas, Periyar.

2. A **common noun** refers to a class of people, places, and things in general. Common nouns are only capitalized when they begin sentences or are used in the names of titles of something.

    Country, students, river, lion.

3. A **concrete noun** refers to people or things that exist physically and that at least one of the senses can detect.

   Cat, oil, desk

4. An **abstract noun** refers to ideas, qualities, concepts, and emotions. They have no physical existence. So we cannot see, touch, hear, smell or taste it.

   Love, fear, humour, time.

5. A **collective noun** refers to a set or group of people, animals, or things.

   Team, crowd, flock, herd

6. A **compound noun** refers to two or more words that join together to make a single noun. They can be written as one word, joined by a hyphen or written as separate words.

   Toothbrush, bus stop, son–in–law, credit card.
   A noun can belong to more than one type. For example, a toothbrush is a common noun, concrete noun, countable noun and compound noun.

CHAPTER FIVE

Verb

A verb is used to express

- an action done by the person thing.
- a state or condition of a person/thing.
- the fact of someone possessing something.

Verbs are very important in a sentence and these are divided into different classes based on 'form' 'function' or 'meaning'

1. **Action verbs (dynamic verbs)**

It is used to refer to actions. These can refer to physical actions as well as mental actions.

Eat, play, sing, think, memorize

2. **Stative verbs**

It refers to the condition or state of being. These are verbs that show emotions, possession, senses and thoughts. These verbs are not usually used in progressive (continuous) tenses.

Hate, own, smell, believe.

Several verbs can refer to states or actions, depending on the context.

This curry *tastes* delicious. (state)

The baker is *tasting* the cake (action)

3. Regular verbs

When a verb follows a regular pattern of the formation of the past tense with '-ed' and without a vowel change, it is called a regular verb.

Walk walked walked

Talk talked talked

Play played played

Like liked liked

Kill killed killed

4. Irregular verbs

An irregular verb does not form its simple past or past participle by adding '-ed' or 'd' to the base form.

Eat ate eaten

See saw seen

Break broke broken

Feed fed fed

Forget forgot forgotten

5. Linking verbs

A linking verb connects the subject of a sentence to a word or phrase that describes it. So the words such as 'taste', 'sound', 'feel', 'become' and other verbs like 'am', 'is', 'are', 'was', 'were', are linking verbs.

The cheese smells rotten.

She became a popular actress.

6. Auxiliary verbs

Auxiliary verbs are used with other verbs to form voices, tenses and moods of those verbs. The main auxiliary verbs are 'to be', 'to have' and 'to do'. These are known as **primary auxiliaries**. They appear in the following forms.

To Be: am, is, are, was, were, be, being, been.

To Have: has, have, had, having.

To Do: does, do, did, doing.

There are some other auxiliary verbs also, such as, can, could, may, might, will, shall, must, would, should and ought to. These are known as **secondary or modal auxiliaries.**

The most common meaning of modal auxiliaries are:

Can: permission, possibility, ability

May: permission, possibility, blessings, wishes.

Must: necessary, obligation.

Have to: necessity, obligation.

Will, shall: willingness, intention.

Would: willingness, probability.

Should: obligation, necessity.

7. Transitive verbs

A transitive verb is a verb that takes a direct object. To find out the object of the sentence ask a question 'what' or 'to whom' to the main verb. A verb that is capable of yielding an answer to these questions is transitive.

Vinay *gave* me a book.

Children *are playing* cricket.

8. **Intransitive verbs**

A verb that has no object is called an intransitive verbs.
She *slept*.
They have been *playing* since morning.

9. **Finite verbs**

When the verb in a sentence indicates tense and changes according to the number and person of the subject, it is called a finite verb.
She *sells* oranges.
They *sell* oranges.
Teena *sold* oranges.
In these sentences, the verb 'sell' changes according to the subject and also shows tense.

10. **Non-finite verbs**

Non-finite verbs do not change with the number and person of the subject and they do not show the tense.
Malavika wants *to donate* her eyes.
We are ready *to go*.
Non-finite verbs are of three kinds – infinities, participles and gerunds.

• Infinitives

The base form of a verb, not limited by number and person is called an infinitive. It can occur with or without 'to'
Children love *to go* for a picnic.
I am going *to join* the music class.

- Participles

A verb has two participles forms. They are present participle and past participle. We can form the present participle of the verbs by adding *ing* to them.

They are *coming* soon.

The past participle of the verbs is formed by adding ed, en, d, t, or n to them.

Laugh laughed

eat eaten

save saved

feel felt

see seen

- Gerunds

A gerund is a verb that ends in *ing* and functions as a noun. Gerunds are also called verb-noun.

Smoking is injurious to health.

Cycling is a good exercise.

CHAPTER SIX

Types of Pronoun

A pronoun is a word that can replace a noun in a sentence. The various kinds of pronouns are:

1. **Personal pronoun**

   It is used to refer to people and sometimes animals.
   I, we, she, he, it, they.

2. **Possessive pronoun**

   It is used to express possession, ownership, relationship, etc.
   Mine, hers, theirs, yours.

3. **Demonstrative pronoun**

   It is used to point out the objects to which they refer.
   This, that, these, those.

4. **Interrogative pronoun**

   It is used to ask questions.
   Who, whom, which, what, whose.

5. **Reflexive pronoun**

   It is used as the reflexive object of a verb.
   Himself, myself, themselves, itself, ourselves.

6. **Indefinite pronoun**

   It is used to refer to something non-specific.
   Somebody, someone, anybody, anyone, anywhere, everywhere, all.

7. **Reciprocal pronoun**

   It is used to express mutual relationships or actions.
   Each other and one another.

8. **Emphatic pronoun**

   It is used to emphasize the noun or pronoun to which they refer.
   Himself, herself, ourselves.
   She, herself, did it.

9. **Distributive pronoun**

   It refers to persons or things one at a time.
   They are therefore always singular.
   Each, every, either, neither, no one, none.

10. **Relative pronoun**

   It is a pronoun that marks a relative clause.
   Who, whom, whose, which, and that.

Exercise
Insert correct form of the pronoun

1. I do not know the man hit my body.
2. He is a man you can trust.
3. Here is an article is made of wood.
4. This is Tomy you met last year.
5. This is the village I spent my childhood.
6. The letter you wrote never arrived.
7. you say is not true.
8. This is the man stole my purse.
9. He is a man everybody loves.
10. is done cannot be undone.

Answers

1. who
2. whom
3. which
4. whom
5. where
6. which
7. What
8. who
9. whom
10. What

Preposition

A proposition is used with a noun or pronoun to show its relation to some other words or phrases in the sentence. Most prepositions have several definitions, so the meaning changes in different contexts. The relations that prepositions express can be as follows:

    a. time relation

    b. place relation

    c. position relation

    d. state relation

    e. cause relation

    f. purpose relation.

1. I reached home *at* 5 o clock. (time)
2. The book *in* the cupboard. (place)
3. Eva is sitting *between* Chris and Devana. (position)
4. They *are* very happy. (state)
5. They jumped up *for* joy. (cause)
6. He married *for* money. (purpose)

At is used:

1. With the names of small places like villages and smaller towns.

Anila lives at Perumbavoor.

2. To denote a certain moment or point in time.

The music show begins at 4 o'clock.

3. When talking about a particular place or building.

They met at the railway station.

4. For festivals which mark a point in the year.

We last met at Christmas.

5. To talk about age.

My father-in-law retired at the age of 58.

6. To show talent in a particular area.

Joby is good at drawing.
7. With mealtimes.
We shall meet at dinner.
8. To denote a sense of time.
We reached our destination at sunset.
9. With schools and universities.
He is at Cambridge.
10. Before place of work, if a particular place is indicated.
My mother works at the Public Library.
In is used:

1. To denote 'the state of being inside.'

The pen is in the box.

2. For the names of countries and continents.

    My uncle lives in Portugal.

3. Before words that denote a period of time.

    Cricket is played in summer and ice-skating in winter.

4. To denote house or residence.

    Paul lives in a modern house.

5. In front of month and year.

    We first went to London in 1984.

6. Before a place of work, if it is a building.

    My sister works in a hospital.

7. To state a period at the end of which something will happen.

    We shall be ready in a few minutes.

8. To denote parts of the day.

    He goes to library in the evening.

9. To show the total length of time taken for the completion of some activity.

She will complete the painting in a week.
On is used:

1. To indicate that something is on the top of a surface.

    The dinner set is on the table.

2. To denote days and dates.

    He was born on 14th August 1984.

3. To indicate the number of building floors.

    My nephew lives on the 3rd floor of the skyline apartment.

4. For the workplace if it is not a building.

    My next-door neighbour works on an estate.

5. To indicate a device or machine such as a phone or a computer.

    The students have been on the computer since morning.

6. To indicate a part of the body.

    I have a mole on my left hand.

7. To indicate travel 'on foot' and 'two-wheeler'.

    He usually goes to college on a bike.

8. For names of streets and roads.

    My house is on the beach road.
    By is used:

1. To say beside, near, next to or at the side of something.

    The house is by a river.

2. To describe how you travel somewhere.

    My parents often go to church by car.

3. To indicate the doer of the action. (passive voice)

    This beautiful picture was drawn by M F Hussain.

4. To describe how you communicate with someone.

    I will send you a copy of the invoice by post.

5. To express 'not later than or a particular time.'

    You should make payment by tomorrow.
    During is used:

1. To express the idea that a situation continues throughout the whole period.

    We sleep during the night.

2. To express an event that took place within a specified period in a time.

We all stayed inside during the storm.
From is used:

1. To express the origin of something or somebody.

   Columbus was from Portugal.

2. To show the material that something is made of.

   Paper is made from wood.

3. To show the reason for death. (if it is not a disease)

   In Attappady children die from starvation.
   Into is used:

1. To mention a position in or inside something.

   The frog fell into the river.

2. To indicate direction.

   He dived into the water.

3. To show its changing state.

   Milk can be made into curd.
   Confusing prepositions

- Made of is used when talking about the basic material of an object whereas made from is used when talking about the substance used in its production.

The bags are made of leather.
The gloves are made from wool.

- Between is used to show something in the middle of or shared by two people.

  Among is used when we refer to more than two people.
  The old man divided his property between his two sons.
  The old man divided his property among his four sons.

- Beside means next to while besides means in addition to.

  There is a hotel bedside at the temple.
  Godwin knows three languages besides English.

- 'In' usually shows a stationary position while into suggests movement from one place to another.

  Sugar is in the jar.
  The mouse ran into the hole.
  Certain nouns, adjectives, verbs and participles are always followed by particular prepositions.
  Accustomed to
  Abstain from
  Acquainted with
  composed of
  concerned about
  Depart from
  Disappointed with
  Discriminated against
  Divorced from
  Excited about

Interested in

Insist on

Known for

Longed for

Married to

Pleased with

Prepared for

Remind of

Repent of

Stare at

Sympathize with

Tired of

Fill in the blanks with suitable prepositions

1. You should abstain alcohol.
2. We started six the morning.
3. We shall do it pleasure.
4. He spoke me English.
5. Man can never be satisfiedpleasure.
6. He married Veena.
7. I prefer coffee tea.
8. I came home taxi.
9. He died fever.
10. She has great regardhim.

Answers

1. from
2. at, in
3. with
4. to, in
5. with
6. to

7. to
8. by
9. of
10. for

CHAPTER EIGHT

Conjunction

Conjunctions are words that join two or more words, phrases or sentences together.

1. Alphin *and* Noble are friends.

2. *When we met*, he advised me to consult a doctor.

3. The teacher is teaching *and* the students are listening.

Conjunctions are of two kinds – coordinating conjunctions and subordinating conjunctions.

Coordinating conjunctions

A conjunction that connects words, clauses or sentences of equal rank or order is called a coordinating conjunction.

Coordinating conjunctions are of four kinds

1. Cumulative or copulative
2. Adversative
3. Disjunctive or alternative
4. Illative

1. **Cumulative or copulative conjunction**

They merely add one statement to another. The most common cumulative conjunctions are and, also, both..... and, not only...., but also, as well as

The blind man got up and walked away slowly.

Rahul as well as his friends are coming.

2. Adversative conjunctions

It is used to express the contrast between two statements. But, still, however, yet, whereas, never are the most common adversative conjunctions.

She is ill but she did not take a rest.

Jacob is rich whereas his brother is poor.

3. Alternative or disjunctive conjunctions

Conjunctions that express alternatives or a choice are called disjunctive conjunction. Or, nor, else, either....or, neither, neither....or, otherwise are the common alternative conjunctions.

Neither a borrower nor a lender is.

You can either come with me to the cinema or walk home.

4. Illative conjunctions

Some conjunctions express something inferred from another statement of fact. These are called illative conjunction.

Examples are: *so*, then, therefore, for....

She is very tired, so she has to take a rest.

He may not be there, *for* his car is not there.

Conjunctions that are used in pairs are called **correlative conjunctions**.

Either.... Or, neither.... nor, both-and, not only.... but also....

Subordinating conjunction

Conjunction that joins a subordinate clause to the main clause is called subordinative conjunction. Some of the most common subordinative conjunctions are because, as, when, whenever, though, until, since and so that.

There are eight main classes of conjunctions, categorized by meaning: time, place, purpose, condition, cause/reason, contrast, effect and comparison.

Time

Time-related conjunctions established a period when the main clause will be or was performed. Conjunctions such as *when, as soon as, before, until, while, after and till* showtime.

Mohan had completed his file before it was time for lunch.

Place

Subordinative conjunctions such as *where and wherever* determine where activities might occur.

You can sit wherever you like.

Purpose

Some subordinative conjunctions such as *in order that* and *so that* indicates purpose.

The teacher spoke slowly so that she could be clearly understood.

Condition

It connects the dependent and independent clauses by showing that the main idea depends on the supporting details. These are indicated by *if, even if, in case, provided that and unless.*

If it rains tomorrow, our match will be cancelled.

Cause or reason

These subordinating conjunctions express a reason as to why something happened and words such as *since, as* and *because* are used for this subordinating.

The rivers are overflowing because we had heavy rains for three days.

Concession

It is used to express an action that took place despite an obstacle. Conjunctions such as *though, although, even if* and *however* are used for this.

We enjoyed the trip although the weather was bad.

Effect

It is used to express the result or consequence. Subordinating conjunctions such as *so-that and such that* indicate effect.

It rained *so* heavily *that* we stayed indoors.

Comparison

It is used to connect the dependent and independent clauses by comparing the two of them. Some subordinating conjunctions such as *then, as-as, as much as* and *no less than* show comparison.

Jupiter is bigger than Saturn.

CHAPTER NINE

Types of Sentences

1. **Simple sentences**

A simple sentence has only one subject and one predicate (verb).
A simple sentence is also called an *independent clause*
I met him yesterday
He went to the hospital

2. **Compound sentences**

A compound sentence has two or more independent clauses joined by a coordinator.
The coordinators are For, And, Nor, But, Or, Yet and So
He went to the hospital <u>and</u> visited his friend.
You can take a taxi <u>or</u> you will become late.

3. **Complex sentence**

A complex sentence has an independent clause and one or more dependent clauses. The word used to link an independent clause is called a subordinating conjunction. The most common subordinating conjunctions are "although, because, before, even though, if, since, until and then." Relative pronouns like who, what and which are also used to connect them.

Even though the exam was difficult, all the students passed.

I know the person who plays the piano in the church choir.

4. Compound complex sentence

A compound-complex sentence contains two independent clauses and at least one dependent clause.

If it rains tomorrow, we shall sit indoors, so we can complete our pending works.

CHAPTER TEN

Clauses

A group of words that contains a subject and a verb is called a clause.

1. Independent clause

It is a clause that can stand on its own as a sentence. It is also known as the main clause.

I went to school.

2. Dependent clause

It doesn't make sense on its own as a sentence. It is also known as the subordinate clause.

Though I wasn't feeling well, I went to school.

Types of depended clauses

- **Noun clause**

A group of words with a subject-verb combination that works as a noun in a sentence is known as the noun clause. It always starts with the following conjunctions: 'what', 'whatever, 'when,' 'which,' 'whichever,' 'who,' 'whoever,' 'whom,' 'that,' 'where,' 'why' and 'how'

There are five different functions that a noun clause can serve: Subject, object, direct object, indirect object, objects of the proposition and subject complements

1. No one knows *who he is* (subjects)
2. I do not know *what he wants* (direct object)
3. She chose to photograph *whoever was willing to pose for her* (indirect object)
4. I am not responsible for *what he does* (Object of the proposition)
5. She runs so fast *that she can outturn her dog* (subject complement)

* **Adverb clause**

It is a clause that works or acts as an adverb in a sentence. It modifies the verb in the sentence. It also modifies an adjective and an adverb sometimes.
Types of adverb clauses

* **Adverb clause of time**

It states when something happens or how often. It often starts with one of the following subordinating conjunctions like 'after, as, as long as, as soon as, before, no sooner than, since, until, when or till.
As soon as the chief minister arrived, the meeting started.
I will remember your help *as long as I live.*

* **Adverb clause of place**

It states where something happens. It is introduced by the subordinating conjunctions like where, wherever, anywhere and everywhere.

You can sit *wherever you like.*

I am coming to meet you *where we met last week.*

- **Adverb clause of manner**

It states how something is done. It often starts with one of the following subordinates conjunctions: 'as', 'like' or 'the way'.

He behaves as if he were mad.

Do as he tells you.

- **Adverb clause of degree – comparison**

It states to what degree something is done or offers a comparison. It often starts with one of the following subordinating conjunctions: 'than", 'as...as', 'so...as', or 'the...the'.

He is *as* tall *as* his father.

It was *so* hot *that* we have to stay inside.

- **Adverb clause of reason – cause**

It offers a reason for the main idea. It is introduced by conjunctions like as, since, because etc.

He could not attend the meeting as he was suffering from a fever.

I don't like him because he is a liar.

- **Adverb clauses of concession**

It offers a statement that contrasts with the main idea. It starts with subordinates like though, although, even

though, while, whereas, if, even if etc.
Even though he worked hard he failed the examination.
That dress is very nice, though I don't like the price.

• **Adverb clause of purpose**

A clause that tells you about the purpose of the verb in the main clause is called the adverb clause of purpose. It is introduced by so that or in order that or lest.
I opened the door so that anybody could come in.
I went to Canada in order that I might earn some money.

• **Relative clause (adjectival clause)**

A group of words that has a subject-verb combination, and acts as an adjective in a sentence is known as a relative clause. An adjectival clause is joined to another clause using relative pronouns like who, whom, that, whose, which, to whom etc.
This is the bag *that I bought yesterday.*
The movie *which we watched last night* was amazing.
Name the clauses in the following sentences

1. The picture which I bought yesterday is very beautiful.
2. My parents were happy because I won the first prize.
3. This is the girl who gave me chocolates yesterday.
4. Although he is very rich, he is a miser.
5. The workers need to know what they should do.
6. The book which is on the table is mine.
7. The beggar seemed as if he hadn't eaten anything for a week.
8. They went to the beach so that they could enjoy the sunset.

9. The man whom you met yesterday is my friend.
10. I believe him because he never lies never tells lies.

Answers:

1. Relative clause.
2. Adverb clause of reason.
3. Relative clause.
4. Adverb clause of concession.
5. Noun clause.
6. Relative (adjectival) clause.
7. Adverb clause of manner.
8. Adverb clause of purpose.
9. Relative (adjectival) clause.
10. Adverb clause of reason.

CHAPTER ELEVEN

Tenses

The term tense refers to the form of the verb indicating the time of the action

or state and its degree of completeness. There are mainly 3 tenses such as

1. Present tense
2. Past tense
3. Future tense

Present Tense

a. **Simple present tense**

Form: S + V1 + O
Simple Present is used:

1. To express habitual action.

She *brushes* her teeth twice a day.
My brother *goes* to the gym every day.
George *feeds* his pets early in the morning.

2. To express universal truths.

The sun *rises* in the east.

Water *boils* at 100 degree Celsius.
Dogs *are* faithful.

3. To express a future event that is part of a fixed programme.

Your exam *starts* at 9.00.AM.
The train *leaves* at 7.30.

b. **Present continuous tense**

Form: S+ am/is/are+ V+ing+ object.

1. It shows activities in progress at the time of speaking.

He is reading a novel.
They *are playing* on the ground.
I *am drawing* a picture.

2. It is also used to express an action in the near future.

She *is leaving* for London tomorrow.
We *are eating* at Café Browne tonight.

c. **Present perfect tense**

Form: S + has/have + V3 + object

1. It shows an action that has just been completed.

I *have lost* my keys.
She *has* just *gone* out.

Scientists *have* recently *discovered* medicine for Covid-19.

2. It is also used for action in the past whose time is not specified.

   I *have visited* Paris.

3. An action that occurred in the past, but as a result in the present.

   We *have lived* here for 10 years.
   I *have known* Mr. Rahul for a long time.

d. **Present perfect continuous tense**

   Form: S+ has/have+ V+ ing+ object
   1. This tense is used for an action that began in the past and is still
   continuing.
   She *has been working* in that college since 2017.
   I *have been studying* for three hours.
   2. This tense is also used for a past action recently completed.
   I am tired because I *have been running*.
   He *has been working* too hard today.

Past Tense

a. **Simple past tense**

   Form: S+V2 +object
   This tense is used for:

1. A past action is done or completed at a particular time in the past.

   I *saw* a film yesterday.
   Mary *arrived* last night.

2. A habitual action in the past.

   She *played* the piano when she was a child.

b. **Past continuous tense**

   Form: S + was/were + verb + ing + object
   This tense is used to convey the idea of a continuing action in the past.
   It *was raining* at 4'0 clock.
   She *was reading* a novel.

c. **Past perfect tense**

   Form: S + had + V3 + object
   This shows an action that took place before another action in the past. This tense talks about the 'past in the past.
   When I reached the station, the train *had left*.
   The patient *had died* before the doctor arrived.

d. **Past perfect continuous tense**

   Form: S + had + been + v + ing + object
   This tense shows an action that continued for some time in the past and ended before another action in the past.
   He *had been working* in a college before he went abroad.

It *had been snowing* since morning, so I stayed inside.

Future Tense

a. **Simple future tense**

Form: S + will/shall +V1 + object

It signifies an arrangement in the near future. It expresses the speaker's intention in the immediate future. We use 'shall' with 1st person [I, we] and 'will' with all other persons.

He *will come* with you tomorrow.

We *shall know* our exam results next week.

b. **Future continuous tense**

Form:S + will/shall + be + V4 + object

It represents an action starting before a point in time and it is going on in the future.

By this time next year, he *will be writing* another book.

I *shall be doing* exercise when you reach home.

c. **Future perfect tense**

Form: S + will/shall/have + V3 + object

It is normally used for an action in the future before another action in the future.

By 4'o clock, *I will have done* my homework.

Sharan *will have arrived* in Canada by this time tomorrow.

d. **Future perfect continuous tense**

Form: S + will/shall/have been + V4

It is used to express an action that will be in progress and will be going on without interruption until a certain point of time in the future.

By May, we *shall have been living* here for two years.

Exercise

1. Abhishek ___________________ yesterday. (arrive)

2. When we finally ___________________ at the camp it ___________________ heavily.

(arrive, rain)

3. I ___________________ this school for the last two years. Before that I ___________________

to St Mary's High School for a year. (attend, go)

.

4.It was a wonderful morning and the sun ___________________ brightly when I ___________________ up. (shine, get)

5. The earth ______ round the sun. (move)

6. It started to rain while we ______ tennis. (are playing, had played, were playing)

7. I ______ English for five years. (studying)

8. I ______ the letter before you arrived. (write)

9.The patient ___________ before the doctor ___________. (die, arrive)

10.I ___________my breakfast in the morning. (have)

11. It for hours. So I cant go out. (rain)

12. Ravi for swimming every Sunday. (go)

13. The taxi for us outside. (wait)

14. We in the canteen tomorrow. (eat)

15. As soon as he the old clock on the wall it again. (repair, break)

16. I my homework when Ram came to see me. (complete)

17. I am sure she the exam. (pass)
18. If you ice, it . (heat, melt)
19.Ihim tomorrow. (see)
20. Every morning she up early. (wake)

Answers

1. arrived
2. arrived, was raining
3. have been attending, went
4. was shining, got
5. moves
6. were playing
7. have been studying
8. had written
9. had died, arrived
10. had
11. has been raining
12. goes
13. is waiting
14. shall eat
15. had repaired, broke
16. had completed
17. will pass
18. heats melts
19. shall see
20. wakes

CHAPTER TWELVE

Articles

There are three articles in the English language 'a' 'an' and 'the'. 'A' and 'an' are known as indefinite articles while 'the' is known as the definite article.

Indefinite articles

We use the indefinite article with singular nouns. It is used to refer to something for the first time. We use 'a' before words that begin with a consonant or consonant sound. We use 'an' before words that begin with a vowel or vowel sound. We do not use indefinite articles before uncountable nouns.

We use indefinite articles

- When the noun is preceded by an adjective.
- A tiger is a dangerous animal
- Paris is a big city

- When we refer to the entire class of something.

A camel can survive without water for many days. (Means all camels, not a specific one)

- The names of professions and occupations take the indefinite article.

My husband is a teacher.
I hope to be an engineer.

- The same rule applies to nouns such as Hero, genius, fool, thief and liar which describe someone by telling us the kind of person he is.

  Don't believe him; he is a liar.

- The indefinite article always follows words 'such' when it is applied to countable things.

  Rahul is such a sincere student.
  Kashmir is such a beautiful place.

- If an article is preceded by so, the indefinite article must be placed between the adjective and the noun.

  I have never come across so barren a field.
  I have never known so hot summer.

- When 'a' is placed before the word few it changes the meaning. Few means not many; a few means 'some.'

  I have a few friends. (A small number of friends).
  I have few friends. (I don't have many friends).
  A few people arrived late. (Some people)
  Few people arrived late. (Not many people)

- There is a similar difference between *little* and *a little*.

  There is little money left-we can't buy that dress.
  There is a little money left-we can buy that dress.

Definite article

We use the definite article.

- To speak about a particular person or thing or one already referred to.

The gold from South Africa is of good quality.

- Before uncountable nouns to give them a specific identity.

The coffee in the kettle is hot.

- Before adjectives when they are used as plural nouns to represent the entire class of something.

The homeless person needs some aid from the government.

- Before the superlative form of adjectives.

Thejus is the tallest boy in my class.

- Before the names of inhabitants of a country collectively community.

The Chinese do not give any importance to religion.

- Before the names of mountain ranges or ranges of hills (but not before single mountains or hills).

The Himalayas, the Alps...(But Mont Blanc, Everest)

- With ordinal numbers.

  Narendra Modi is the 14th prime minister of India.

- Before the names of rivers, canals, seas, oceans, valleys, deserts and forests.

  The Black Forest, the Caribbean Sea, the Sahara, the Panama Canal.

- Before the names of ships and trains.

  The Sabari express left the station.
  The Santa Maria was the first ship used by Christopher Columbus for his exploration.

- Before names of newspapers journals and books.

  I saw an advertisement in 'The Indian express'.
  Have you ever read 'The Odyssey?
  (But we say homer's Odyssey, Valmiki's Ramayana)

- When we speak of unique things or the only ones of their kind.

  The moon is the only natural satellite of the earth.

- Before musical instruments.

  The choir leader was playing the piano.

- Before nouns like ' church', 'prison', 'hospital', 'market' etc when we refer to them as merely buildings.

I am going to the hospital to visit my friend, who is suffering from cancer.

Gopal's mother came to the school to complain about the behaviour of one of the students.

(But we say Gopal goes to school every day.

Note: 'The' is omitted, when the reference is to the purpose for which the building exists).

Exercise

New suitable articles in the sentences below

1. My friend lives in European country.
2. We can trust him because he is honest man.
3. Tom isexpert at mathematics
4. Russia is largest country in the world
5. I want pizza.
6. Ajay is best in this subject.
7. Last night I had strange dream.
8. boy who is playing violin is my friend.
9. My parents live inapartment in city centre.
10. School children in India have to wear uniform.

Answers

1. a
2. an
3. an
4. the
5. a
6. the
7. a
8. the, the
9. an, the
10. a

CHAPTER THIRTEEN

Concord Agreement of Verb and Subject

A verb must agree with its subject in Number and Person. If the sentence is singular, the verb must be singular and if the subject is plural, the verb must be plural.

She goes to church every day.

They go to church every day.

1. When the subject of the sentence is composed of two or more singular nouns or pronouns joint by 'and' requires a plural verb.

    Gold and silver are used for making ornaments

- But when two or more nouns represent a compound name of one thing or suggest one idea to the mind, then the compound is thought of as singular and takes a singular verb.

    Bread and butter is available here.

2. When two or more singular nouns or pronouns are connected by 'or' or 'nor' use a singular verb.

Raji or Meera is going to the party.

3. If in a sentence two singular subjects are connected by either... or neither... nor, we use a singular verb.

    Either Sam or Kumar is teaching you English.
    Neither Mathew nor Johny is coming with us.

4. If in an either/ or neither/ nor sentence one of the subjects is I, use it second and with being.

    Neither Raju nor I am going to Delhi.

5. In a sentence where we have a singular and a plural subject connected by 'or' or 'nor', the verb will depend on the nearer subject. This is also called the rule of proximity.

    The teacher or the students are arranging the books.
    The students or the teacher is arranging the books.

6. Similarly, a singular and a plural subject connected by either... or neither...nor, the verb will depend on the nearer subject.

    Neither John nor his friends are doing any decoration.

7. When the subject of the sentence is a pronoun like 'everybody', 'any one, 'anybody', 'nobody', 'each', 'either', 'neither', 'everyone', 'someone', and 'somebody', we use a singular verb.

    Either of the novels *is* interesting.

Everyone *likes* to drink tea.
Each of the students *dances*very well.

8. In some sentences, words like *besides along with, as well as* etc are used with the main subject. Here, the verb will follow the main subject.

    The captain, along with his crew, is doing exercise there.
    Gold, as well as silver, is very precious metals.

9. When the subject is a sum of money or a period of time, we use a singular verb.

    Thousand rupees was the cost for that picture.
    Thirty minutes is allowed to complete that work.

10. The words 'there' and 'here' are never subjects. When a sentence starts with there or here, the verb follows the noun that comes later.

    There are two options.
    Here is an apple.

11. When pronouns such as 'who', 'that' and 'which' are used, the verb depends on the noun immediately before that verb.

    Vivek is one of the students who were selected for the cricket team.
    Vivek is the boy who was selected for the cricket team.

12. *A lot of* and *plenty of* take a plural verb when they are used for countable nouns: they take a singular verb

when they are used for uncountable nouns.

There are plenty of mangoes in that tree.
There is a lot of enthusiasm among the students.
'A number of means several and is there for always followed by a plural verb.
There have been a number of books on the shelf.

13. A collective noun thought of as a single unit takes a singular verb.

    A troop of monkeys is playing there.

14. Nouns like scissors, trousers, pants, spectacles, shoes and glasses take plural verbs though they refer to single articles. 'A pair of ', when used with these nouns take a singular verb.

    The scissors are in the cupboard.
    This pair of shoes is too costly.

15. If we omit the words 'a pair of' and merely use the plural word, then it must take a plural word.

    The scissors are lying on the table.

16. 'Some of' and 'half of' take a plural verb when used with countable nouns. They take a singular verb when used with uncountable nouns.

    Some of the students are very intelligent.
    Half of the oil in the bottle is finished.

17. When the subject contains the words 'a a dozen' followed by a noun, it takes a plural verb.

    There are a dozen colour pencils in the cupboard.

18. Collective nouns such as team, committee, staff, jury, group, class etc may be singular or plural depending on the way these nouns are used. If it is considered a group, it takes a singular verb, and if the focus is on the individuals in the group, it takes a plural verb.

    The committee gratefully acknowledges the assistance of the volunteers.
    The committee has been arguing among themselves.

19. In English 'more than one' is treated as singular, so we use a singular verb.

    More than one warning was issued to the boys.

20. When the plural noun is a proper name for some singular object such as the title of a book, or the name of a house or a hotel, the verb should be singular.

    'Gulliver's Travels is a masterpiece by Jonathan Swift.
    'Thirty-nine Steps' was written by John Buchan.
    Exercise

    1. There several people in the room. (is/are)
    2. A new car a lot of money. (cast)
    3. Antsvery slowly. (move)
    4. Aeroplanes very fast. (fly)
    5. An aeroplane more quickly than a falcon. (fly)

6. One of the playersfrom the same city as myself. (come)
7. Either she or her friends responsible for this accident. (is/are)
8. Five thousand rupees what it would cost to buy a new wristwatch.(is/are)
9. Neither me nor my parents present there. (was/were)
10. Sheela along with her parents going to hospital. (was/were)
11. Five kilometers __________ too far to walk. (is/are)
12. The teacher with his students_(has/have)
13. Most of my friends musicians. (is,are)
14. He (write) a poem every day.
15. Either George or Thomasthe key to the cupboard. (has/have)
16. The staff decided that classes will not be held on Monday. (has/have)
17. Everyone the answer to the question. (know)
18. One of my three pensmissing. (is/are)
19. The scissorsuseless now. (is/are)
20. The cow as well as the sheep grass. (eat)

Answers

1. are
2. costs
3. move
4. fly
5. flies
6. comes
7. are
8. is
9. were
10. was

11. is
12. has
13. are
14. writes
15. has
16. has
17. knows
18. is
19. are
20. eats

CHAPTER FOURTEEN

Direct and Indirect Speech

Manoj said, "I need a pen."

Manoj said that he needed a pen.

In the first sentence, we quote the words of Manoj. This is called **Direct Speech.** Manoj's words are put within inverted commas or quotation marks. In the second sentence, we report what Manoj said without quoting his exact words.' This is called **Indirect or Reported Speech.**

It may be noticed that in changing the direct speech into indirect speech certain changes have been made.

1. The comma after said and the quotation marks are removed.
2. We have used the conjunction 'that' before the indirect state.
3. The pronoun *I* is changed to *he*
4. The verb *need* is changed to *needed* (present tense is changed into past)

Rules for changing direct into indirect speech

- All present tenses of the direct speech are changed into their past form in the indirect

Simple present – Simple past
Present continuous – past continuous
Present perfect – past perfect
Simple past – past perfect
Past continuous – past perfect continuous
Shall – should/would
Will – would
May – might
Can – could
Must – had to/would have to
Note: the tense cannot change if the statement is still relevant or if it is a universal truth.
The teacher said, "The earth goes around the sun."
The teacher said that the earth goes around the sun.

- Change in place and time

Today – that day
Tomorrow – next day/following day
Yesterday – the previous day/the day before/ the last day
Last week/month – previous week/month
Next week/month – the following week/month
Ago – before/earlier
This – that
These – those
Here – there
Now – then
At once – immediately

- Pronouns of 1st and 2nd person become 3rd person while reporting except when the speaker himself is reporting

  I – he/she
  Me - him/her
  My – his/ her
  Mine – his / hers
  Myself – himself/herself
  We – they
  Us – them
  Our – their
  Ours – theirs
  Ourselves – themselves
  You – he / she / we / they / I

- A reported question has the word order of a statement- that is the verb follows the subject. Usually, the reporting verb asked is used.

  The teacher said to me, "what are you doing"?
  The teacher asked me what I was doing.

- In yes or no questions the conjunction 'whether'/ 'if' is used after the reporting verb.

  "Were you present yesterday", the teacher said to Raju.
  The teacher asked Raju whether he had been present the previous day.

- The verb in the imperative sentence is changed into "to-infinitive".

The master said to his servant, "open the door and clean the table at once".

The master ordered his servant to open the door and clean the table immediately.

- While reporting exclamatory sentences the reporting verbs are changed into exclaimed, mourned, wondered, praised etc. The exclamation marks and the words like alas! hurrah! Oh! etc are omitted and the conjunction 'that' is used.

  Mary said, "oh! I am ill".
  Mary cried out that she was very ill.
  John said, "How deep the wound is!"
  John cried out in sorrow that the wound was very deep.

- Conditionals of the second and third types do not change.

  Leela said, "If you plan properly you will succeed in your efforts.
  Leela said that if you plan properly you will succeed in your efforts.

- In Direct and Indirect speech the following verbs do not change.

  Would, should, ought to, might, could
  The teacher said, "They might come again."
  The teacher said that they might come again.

Exercise:
1. "Joseph, have you finished writing", asked the teacher
2. "What are you doing," John asked Mary

3. Aswin asked Shyam, "Whose pen are you writing with"

4. He said to Raju "Please wait there till I return"

5. "Did you see the exhibition", the teacher said to me

6. Manu said, "I shall pay your wages tomorrow."

7. "Workers are repairing the main road," he said.

8. The teacher said, "I have evaluated the answer books".

9. She said, "I have been staying with the Smiths since my arrival here"

10. He said, "A tragic incident happened yesterday

11. He said, "She was watering the roses when I saw her".

12. The teacher said to the boy, "If you do your best you will surely pass"

13. He said, "Alex was swimming in the pool."

14. "I am sure you did your best," said Thomas to me

15. They said, "How happy we are here"

16. "Rani, show me your notebook", said the teacher

17. "When did you return from the office?" asked Leela to her father

18. "You should clean your room every day", said mother.

19. Shahul said, "I am worried about the results."

20. "I saw you in the library yesterday", Parveen said.

Answers:

1. The teacher asked Joseph whether he had finished writing.
2. John asked Mary what he was doing.
3. Aswin asked Shyam whose pen he was writing with.
4. He requested Raju to wait there till he returned.
5. The teacher asked me whether I had seen the exhibition.
6. Manu said that he would pay his wages the next day.

7. He said that workers were repairing the main road.
8. The teacher said that she had evaluated the answer books.
9. She said that she had been staying with the Smiths since her arrival there.
10. He said that a tragic incident had happened the day before.
11. He said that she had been watering the roses when he had seen her.
12. The teacher told the boy that if he does his best he will surely pass.
13. He said that Alex had been swimming in the pool.
14. Thomas told me that he was sure that I had done my best.
15. They exclaimed that they were very happy there.
16. The teacher asked Rani to show her/him her notebook.
17. Leela asked her father when he had returned from the office.
18. The mother advised me to clean my room every day.
19. Shahul said that he was worried about the results.
20. Parveen said that she had seen me (him/her) in the library the previous day.

CHAPTER FIFTEEN

Question Tag

It is common in conversation to attach a question to the end of the statement to ask the opinion of the person to whom it is addressed. We often use question tags when we want to know whether the listener agrees or disagrees with our statement. The chief points to notice are as follows

- We use the same auxiliary verb in the tag as in the main sentence. If there is no auxiliary verb in the main sentence, we use 'do' in the tag.

  Manu is a smart boy, isn't he?
  They completed their work, didn't they?

- A positive statement takes a negative question tag and a negative statement takes a positive question tag.

  You can swim, can't you?
  They aren't going out, are they?
  Little, few, hardly, scarcely, rarely, seldom, etc. are treated as negative and take the positive tag.
  A few, a little are treated as positive and take a negative question tag.
  Barking dogs seldom bite, do they?

- The pronoun is to be used in the question tag and it depends on the subject of the sentence.

  Any singular inanimate subject -- it
  Any plural inanimate subject -- They
  Everybody / Everyone -- They
  One of us -- We
  Some of us -- We
  None of you -- You
  Some of you – You
  One -- one

- Everybody, everyone, no one, nobody is singular. So we use a singular verb and singular pronoun with them, but in the question tag, a plural verb and plural pronoun will be used.

  Everybody has to come early, haven't they?

- A suggestion that begins with let us take the tag -- shall we.

  Let's go out, shall we

- Question tags commonly used after imperatives are will you, won't you, would you, can you, can't you etc. They are not questions but just another way of saying please.

  Have another cup of tea, will you?
  Use common sense, can't you?
  Be careful when you cross the road, won't you?
  Remember to lock the door, won't you?

Note: Since 'won't you' suggests urgency, it is the form of the tang used with entreaties or requests that have the force of entreaties.

- For imperative sentences beginning with 'let' but not followed by us, the question tag will be, 'will you.'

  Let them do their work, will you?
  Let Ramu go, will you?

- For sentences having nothing, anything, something, everything as the subject, the question tag will have 'it' as the pronoun.

  Everything was wrong, wasn't it?

- In exclamatory sentences, the question tag will contain auxiliary verbs.

  How beautiful the monument is, isn't it?

- If the subject of a sentence is there /one/this/that/ these/those then the question tag will contain there/ one/this etc as the pronoun.

  There are some biscuits in the box, aren't there?
  One cannot find a solution to this problem, can one?

- After 'I am' the tag used is 'aren't' I '. 'I am not' takes the tag 'am I '.

  I am taller than you, aren't I?
  I am not lazy, am I?

Exercise

Add the appropriate tag in the following sentences

1. The book is rare now, ?
2. The journey was not an easy one, ?
3. Let her come in, ?
4. I never drink tea, ?
5. You like him, ?
6. They will go home soon,?
7. The dress was not too expensive, ?
8. Let's go and play now,?
9. We have plenty of time,?
10. None of the food was wasted,?
11. Few people knew the answer,?
12. A few people knew the answer,?
13. I am older than you,?
14. Pass me the newspaper,?
15. He looks dishonest,?
16. We mustn't be late,?
17. We could go for a trip,?
18. We haven't had our lunch at,?
19. She looks very beautiful,?
20. I hardly saw him,?

Answer

1. isn't it
2. was it
3. will you
4. do I
5. don't you
6. will they
7. was it

8. shall we
9. haven't we
10. was it
11. did they
12. didn't they
13. aren't I
14. will you
15. doesn't he
16. must we
17. couldn't we
18. have we
19. doesn't she
20. did I

CHAPTER SIXTEEN

Active and Passive Voice

The voice of a verb tells us whether the subject does an action or it is the receiver of the action's effect. Voice is of two kinds- active and passive.

A verb is in active voice when its form shows that this subject is the doer of the action.

Edison invented the Gramophone.

A verb is in the passive voice when its form shows that *something is done to* the person or thing denoted by the subject.

The gramophone was invented by Edison.

Voice is the form of a verb that shows whether what is denoted by the subject *does something or has something done to it.*

We can change a verb in the active voice into a passive voice provided that the verb has an object.

Voice

How to convert an active voice into passive voice

1. Find out the object of the given sentence and make the object a subject

2. According to the subject and tense of the verb use one of the forms of the verb 'to be'

    Simple Present – Am / is /are
    Simple Past – Was/ Were
    Continuous – being
    Perfect tense – been
    {Will/ Shall/ Can/ Could
    May/ Might/ Should/ Would} - be

3. After one of the forms of the verb "to be" use the past participle of the main verb of the given sentence
4. Make the subject of the given sentence as the object in the passive voice

    <u>Subject</u><u>Object</u>
    I Me
    We Us
    He Him
    She Her
    They Them

Simple Present

S+ is/ am/ are + V3 + by + O

She writes a poem.
   A poem is written by her
   He drinks tea
   Tea is drunk by him

They play cricket
Cricket is played by them

Present continuous

S + am/ is/ are + being + V3 + by + o

Mohan is drawing a picture.
    A picture is being drawn by Mohan.
    They are selling Mangoes.
    Mangoes are being sold by them.
    They are eating an apple.
    An apple is being eaten by them.

Present Perfect

S + has/ have + been + V3 + by + O

They have sold the house
    The house has been sold by them
    He has drawn many pictures
    Many pictures have been drawn by him
    They have asked us to be there at 5 o'clock
    We have been asked to be there at 5 o'clock

Simple past

S + was / were + V3 + by + O

The minister made a speech
   A speech was made by the minister
   He sold his cow
   His cow was sold by him
   He saw a film yesterday
   A film was seen by him yesterday
   People took the injured person to the hospital
   The injured person was taken to the hospital
   Nobody invited him
   He was not invited

Past Continuous

S + was/were+ being + V3 + by + O

The girls were cleaning the floor
   The floor was being cleaned by the girls
   They were building a bridge
   A bridge was being built
   They were polishing in the shoes
   The shoes were being polished
   She was writing novels
   Novels were being written by her

Past Perfect

   S + had been + V3 +by+ O
   Roy had finished the project before the deadline.

The project had been finished before the deadline by Roy.

They had not invited me to the party.

I had not been invited to the party.

<u>Simple future</u>

S+ will/shall+be+V3+by+o

We shall discuss the matter tomorrow.

The matter will be discussed by us tomorrow.

He will meet the manager next week.

The manager will be met by him next week.

<u>Future Perfect</u>

S+ will/shall+ have been+V3+by+o

They will have spent the money.

The money will have been spent by them.

They will have built a bridge across the river.

A bridge will have been built across the river.

He will have finished the work by the end of the June

The work will have been finished by the end of June

<u>Modal Verbs</u>

Should, would, can, could, may, might, ought to, must, used to, need, has to, have to, had to are the modal verbs.

S+ modal + be + V3 + by + o

He may buy a car.

A car may be bought by him.

You need not punish the boy.

The boy need not be punished by you.

He might do the work.

The work might be done by him.
They have to finish the work.
The work has to be finished by them.
You must not punish her.
She must not be punished by you.
The officer has to interview the candidates.
The candidates have to be interviewed by the officer.
Exercise:
Change the following sentences into passive voice.

1.   Ani has made this painting.
2.   The army builds the bridge.
3.   The students planted a few saplings today
4.   When will they open the registration counter.
5.   Some boys were helping the old women.
6.   Columbus discovered America.
7.   They sell mangoes here.
8.   The dramatic club enacted a play today.
9.   They are repairing the old building.
10. I have finished my homework.

Answers:
1.This painting has been made by Ani.
2. The bridge is built by the army.
3. A few saplings were planted today by the students.
4. When the registration counter will be opened by them?
5. The old woman was being helped by some boys.
6. America was discovered by Columbus.
7. Mangoes are sold here by them.
8. A play was enacted by the dramatic club today.

9. The old building is being repaired.
10. My homework has been finished.
Change the following sentences into active voice.

1. Tamil is spoken by the people of Tamil Nādu.
2. The letter was posted by me on Monday.
3. The door was being made by the carpenter.
4. The tiger was shot by the hunter.
5. Our food is cooked by our mother.
6. The flag will be hoisted by the principal.
7. How were the windows broken by the thief?
8. Let the door be opened.
9. Can English be spoken by him?
10. A picture is being drawn.

Answers
1. The people of Tamil Nadu speak Tamil.
2. I posted the letter on Monday.
3. The carpenter was making the door.
4. The hunter shot the tiger.
5. Mother cooks our food.
6. The principal will hoist the flag.
7. How did the thief break the windows.
8. Open the door.
9. Can he speak English.
10. The artist is drawing a picture.

Imperative sentences

Let + object + be + V3
Close the door.
Let the door be closed.
Give the answer.
Let the answer be given.

Punish the culprit
Let the culprit be punished.
Translate it into English.
Let it be translated into English.
<u>Interrogative sentences</u>
[Step 1. Convert the interrogative sentence into a statement.
Step 2. Write its passive form.
Step 3. Convert that statement into an interrogative.]

1. Did he give you my textbook?

    [He gave you, my textbook.
    My textbook was given to you by him.]
    Was my textbook given to you by him?

2. Did you grow these flowers in your garden?

    [You grew these flowers in your garden.
    These flowers were grown in your garden.]
    Were these flowers grown in your garden?

3. Do you see coconut trees in Arabia?

    [You see coconut trees in Arabia.
    Coconut trees are seen in Arabia.]
    Are coconut trees seen in Arabia?

4. Will you buy an encyclopedia?

    [You will buy an encyclopedia.
    An encyclopedia will be bought by you]
    Will an encyclopedia be bought by you?

Change the voice of the following sentences

1. The police have arrested the thief.
2. The game was spoiled by the young man.
3. They will finish the work in a fortnight.
4. We compelled the enemy to surrender.
5. He was elected as the president by them.
6. Clean the table.
7. Did anyone laugh at you?
8. They will have to question you.
9. Will you complete the novel this month?
10. The children are singing a beautiful song.

Answers

1. The thief has been arrested.
2. The young man spoiled the game.
3. The work will be finished in a fortnight.
4. The enemy was compelled to surrender by us.
5. They elected him president.
6. Let the table be cleaned.
7. Were you laughed at by anyone?
8. You will have to be questioned.
9. Will the novel be completed by you this month.
10. A beautiful song is being sung by the children.

CHAPTER SEVENTEEN

Conditionals

A conditional sentence states that something will happen if a condition is fulfilled. There are four different types of conditional sentences in English. Each expresses a different degree of probability that a situation will occur or would have occurred under certain circumstances

1. Zero conditional
2. First conditional
3. Second conditional
4. Third conditional

Zero conditional sentences express general truths. It means that a result is a certainty if the condition is fulfilled.

if + ... (simple present) .... +..... (simple present) ....

If it rains, the plants get wet.

If you heat ice, it melts

The **first conditional sentences** are used to express situations in which the outcome is highly likely to happen in the future.

if + ... (simple present) ..... + ... will

If you work hard, you will achieve your goal.

My daughter will cry if she watches this movie.

The **second conditional sentences** are used to express outcomes that are unrealistic or unlikely.

if + ... (simple past) .... + ... Would ....

If I owned an aircraft, I would let people fly without any fare.

If I were rich, I would never work again.

The **third conditional sentences** are used to explain that present circumstances would be different if something different had happened in the past

if + ... had .... + ... would have ....

If they had arrived half an hour earlier, they would have attended the meeting.

If our team had played well, we would not have lost the match.

Exercise

Complete the following sentences by choosing the correct options:

1. If she saw a snake,

a. she will be terrified.
b. she would be terrified.

2. You will succeed in your efforts if you

a. plan properly.
b. had planned properly.

3. If he studies hard,

a. he will pass the exam.
b. he would pass the exam.

4. We would have arrived on time

a. if we left earlier.
b. if he had left earlier.

5. If children eat a lot of candy,

a. They get sick.
b. They will get sick.
c.

Answers
1.b,
2.a,
3.a,
4.b,
5.a

CHAPTER EIGHTEEN

Degrees of Comparison

The degree of comparison speaks to the three forms of adjectives that can be used when comparing items. When we want to compare two or more nouns with the same attribute, we can change the form of adjectives to show comparison. These forms are called degrees of comparison. There are three degrees of comparison.

1. Positive degree
2. Comparative degree
3. Superlative degree

Positive degree

The positive degree of an adjective is the simplest form of the adjective. It is used to denote the mere existence of some quality.

Steve is as tall as his brother.

He is as smart as his cousin.

Comparative degree

The comparative degree of an adjective is used to compare two nouns with the same quality. The comparative form of adjectives is made either by adding the suffix 'er' to them or the word 'more' before them. We use 'than' or 'to' the comparative degree of adjectives.

Steve is taller than William.

My sister Maya is elder to me by three years.

Superlative degree

It is used when we compare more than two nouns. The superlative form of adjectives is made either by adding the suffix 'est' to them or the word 'most' before them. We use the definite article 'the' before the superlative degree.

Steve is the tallest boy in the class.

Russia is the largest country in the world.

- If we compare one thing with others of its kind that we know, then we are comparing amongst many things, and so we need a superlative.

This is the most interesting novel I have ever read.

Note: When we compare qualities in the same person or thing we do not use the 'er' form of comparative degree but use the form of 'more'.

Changing the degree of comparison

For most adjectives of one syllable, and a few of more than one syllable, we can form the comparative degree by adding 'er' and the superlative degree by adding 'est' to the positive degree.

bright brighter brightest

clean cleaner cleanest

sharp sharper sharpest

old older oldest

slow slower slowest

When the positive degree ends in 'e', we add only 'r' and 'st'.

wise wiser wisest

late later latest

white whiter whitest

fierce fiercer fiercest

strange stranger strangest

When the positive degree ends in 'y', preceded by a consonant, we change the 'y' into 'I' before adding 'er' and 'est'.

dirty dirtier dirtiest

lovely lovelier loveliest

happy happier happiest

healthy healthier healthiest

pretty prettier prettiest

ugly uglier ugliest

When a one-syllable word ends in a single consonant, preceded by a short vowel, we double the consonant before adding 'er' and 'est'.

wet wetter wettest

hot hotter hottest

fat fatter fattest

big bigger biggest

flat flatter flattest

Adjectives of more than two syllables form the comparative and superlative degrees with 'more' and 'most' before the positive degrees.

Important more important most important

difficult more difficult most difficult

diligent more diligent most diligent

renowned more renowned most renowned

careless more careless most careless

Some adjectives do not follow any fixed rules to form the comparative and superlative degrees.

bad worse worst

much more most

little less least

far further/ farther furthest/ farthest

good better best

Some adjectives suggest that something is only one of its kind. Such adjectives do not change their degree.

Exercise:

Filling the blanks with correct form adjectives.

1. No other girl is as as Rakhi (bright)
2. A train is than a car. (fast)
3. Of the two brothers, the was the (young, clever)
4. This is of all the books that I have read ever before. (funny)
5. Who is the pupil in your class. (tall)
6. My little sister is the in the family. (short)
7. Bincy is of all the four sisters. (beautiful)
8. You will have to do your work than this. (carefully)
9. Alfred is the person in the village. (rich)
10. No other planet is as as the Jupiter (big)

Answers:

1. bright
2. faster
3. younger, cleverer
4. the funniest
5. tallest
6. shortest
7. the most beautiful
8. more carefully
9. richest
10. big

change the degree of comparison without changing the meaning.

1. Paris is the most expensive place to live in the world.
2. Rebecca is more intelligent than any other girl in the class.
3. No other country in this world is as big as Russia.
4. Alex is stronger than any other boy in the group.

Answers:

1. No other place in the world is as expensive to live in as Paris. (positive)

   Paris is more expensive than any other place to live in the world. (comparative)

2. Rebecca is the most intelligent girl in the class. (superlative)

   No other girl in the class is as intelligent as Rebecca. (positive)

3. Russia is bigger than any other country in the world (comparative)

   Russia is the biggest country in the world. (superlative)

4. No other boy in the group is as strong as Alex. (positive)

   Alex is the strongest boy in the group. (superlative)

CHAPTER NINETEEN

Phrasal Verbs

A phrasal verb comprises a verb and a preposition or an adverb and is used to denote an action just like a verb. The meaning of a verb changes when it is combined with different prepositions.

Some common phrasal verbs

1. Account for: to destroy, to kill.
2. Allow for: to take into consideration.
3. Break into: to enter by force.
4. Break off: to stop.
5. Break out: to happen suddenly.
6. Breakthrough: to force a way through.
7. Break up: to put an end to.
8. Bring down: make unhappy.
9. Bring up: raise a child.
10. Call of: cancel.
11. Catch the eye: to attract attention
12. Count on: rely on.
13. Chip in: to interrupt a conversation
14. Cut in: interrupt
15. Do away with: to put an end.
16. Drop-in: to be sit.
17. Figure out: find the answer.

18. Get at: to reach
19. Get back at: take revenge
20. Get over: overcome a problem.
21. Give away: reveal a secret.
22. Give up: to stop doing something.
23. Go off: to explode
24. Hand in: submit.
25. Hand out: to distribute to a group of people.
26. Hand on: to pass on from one person to another.
27. Iron out: to resolve differences
28. Lay off: to stop employing.
29. Let down: to disappoint.
30. Let off: to allow to go without punishment.
31. Look after: to care for.
32. Make out: to understand.
33. Nail down: to identify something exactly
34. Nod off: to fall asleep
35. Pass away: die
36. Put about: to spread.
37. Put down: to suppress, to insult
38. Put in: to do.
39. Put off: to postpone
40. Put on: to dress oneself
41. Run into: meet unexpectedly
42. Runout: to be finished
43. Set about: to start
44. Sort out: organize
45. Take after: resemble
46. Turn down: decrease the volume or strength/ refuse
47. Turn off: switch off
48. Turn up: appear suddenly
49. Win over: to persuade

50. Wink at: to pretend not to notice

CHAPTER TWENTY

Idioms and Phrases

An idiom is a combination of words that has a meaning which is different from its literal meaning.

Idioms and phrases

A hard nut to crack - A very difficult problem

An apple of one's eye – something/someone very precious or dear

A square meal – A nutritious meal

At arm's length – at a safe distance

Have an ax to grind – have a private reason for doing something

See eye to eye - agreeing with someone

Pride of place - Predominant position

Bee in one's bonnet - Obsessed with something & talk about it constantly

A cat on hot bricks - Very nervous

Dog eat dog situation – A situation of fierce competition

Once in a blue moon – very rarely

Keep the wolf from the door – To avoid starvation

Play duck and drakes – Spend money carelessly

To cost an arm and a leg - very expensive

Let the cat out of the box – reveal a secret

Break a leg – good luck

Call it a day – stop working

Giving someone the cold shoulder – to ignore someone
At one's beck and call - subject to one's will
Turn a deaf ear – to ignore
To make do - to manage with what is available
To nip the bud – to cut off in the earliest stage
Down to earth – sensible and realistic
Kick the bucket – die
Last straw: the final problem in a series of problems
Forty winks - a short nap
All wet – completely mistaken
When pigs fly – something that never happens
A piece of cake – something very easy to do
To rain cats and dogs – heavy rain

CHAPTER TWENTY-ONE

Correct the Sentences

1. This car is belonging to me.
2. Ganges is a sacred river.
3. Bread and butter are what we had today.
4. Every child have been given chocolates.
5. Either Kennedy or Stalin have done this.
6. Politics are not included in the syllabus
7. One must respect his teacher.
8. He likes to live in open air.
9. Albert is wiser than any other student in the class.
10. They were believing in ghosts.
11. He went to church to see the vicar.
12. The smuggler was sent to the prison.
13. I expected that he will complete the work.
14. She neither speaks Japanese nor English.
15. The bangles are made from gold.
16. My brother is on the Army.
17. Can I have a chocolate?
18. He congratulated me for my success.
19. He is owing two apartments.
20. Lakshmi distributed the sweets between her three friends.
21. I go to the school by bus.

22. The answers should be written by ink.
23. Rahul as well as his friends are coming.
24. Mangoes which I bought yesterday was very sweet.
25. My nephew, besides his friends, were participating in that programme.

Answers

1. This car belongs to me.
2. The Ganges is a sacred river.
3. Bread and butter are what we had today.
4. Every child has been given chocolates.
5. Either Kennedy or Stalin has done this.
6. Politics is not included in the syllabus
7. One must respect one's teacher.
8. He likes to live in the open air.
9. Albert is the wisest student in the class.
10. They believed in ghosts.
11. He went to the church to see the vicar.
12. The smuggler was sent to prison.
13. I expected that he would complete the work.
14. She speaks neither Japanese nor English.
15. The bangles are made of gold.
16. My brother is in the Army.
17. Can I have a piece of/bar of chocolate?
18. He congratulated me on my success.
19. He is owing to two apartments.
20. Lakshmi distributed the sweets among her three friends.
21. I go to school by bus.
22. The answers should be written in ink.
23. Rahul as well as his friends are coming.
24. The mangoes which I bought yesterday were very sweet.

25. My nephew, besides his friends, was participating in that programme.

CHAPTER TWENTY-TWO

Punctuation

Punctuation marks commonly used in English are as follows:

1. Full stop (period) .
2. Comma ,
3. Apostrophe '
4. Semicolon ;
5. Colon :
6. Brackets [ ]
7. Parentheses ( )
8. Quotation mark " "
9. Hypen -
10. Dash _
11. Ellipsis point ...
12. Exclamation mark !
13. Question mark ?
14. Slash /

1. **Full stop (period)**

a. Commonly used at the end of declarative sentences.

Hamlet is written by Shakespeare.

b. After an abbreviation.

    B.C. Before Christ
    U.K. United Kingdom

2. Comma

a. Use commas to separate items in a series except the last two.

    Pen, pencils, eraser, sharpener and instruments box.

b. Use a comma before coordinating conjunctions when they join independent clauses.

    He worked hard, but he failed in the examination.

c. To mark off a direct quotation from the rest of the sentence.

    "You should complete your homework by tomorrow," said the teacher.

d. Use a comma to set off a noun of direct address.

    "Shiju, please give me a pen".

e. After a participle phrase with which a sentence begins.

    Sitting at the shade of a tree, the young boy was reading a novel.

f. To separate an adverbial clause at the beginning of a sentence.

When I reached the station, the train had left.

g. Use a comma after introductory words, phrases and clauses.

"Yes, she looks gorgeous"

h. Use a comma before and after non- restrictive words.

Her elder son, Sam, flew to Mumbai.
(Note: non-restrictive words are not essential to the meaning of the sentences).

3. **Apostrophe**

a. Use an apostrophe to indicate that some letters have been omitted from a word.

Doesn't does not
Shan't shall not
It's it is

b. To form the possessive case.

Boys' hostel
Children's Park
Kevin's mother

4. **Semicolon**

a. Use a semicolon to separate two complete thoughts, when these parts are not joined together by coordinating conjunctions.

I was busy yesterday; I couldn't complete the project.

b. Use a semicolon in a series when the parts already a have commas within them.

The meeting was conducted by John Mathew, president of the club; Philip Augustin, secretary of the club; and all the board of directors.

5. **Colon**

a. Use a colon before a list of items.

I bought four novels: Dr Faustus, The Midnight Children, King Lear and The Alchemist.

b. Use a colon before a long, formal statement or quotation.

Shakespeare's Macbeth starts with these famous words: "Fair is Foul and Foul is Fair.."

6. **Brackets**

a. Brackets are used for explanatory comments or to clarify meanings.

He [Mr. Alfred] was the only person present at the time of the robbery.

7. Parentheses

a. Use parentheses to set off ideas that are added to a sentence but are not considered of major importance.

My niece Jordhana (8 years old) draws beautiful pictures in her school newspaper.

b. Periods, quotation marks and exclamation marks go inside the parentheses if they belong in the material in parentheses and go outside the parenthesis if they go with the rest of the sentences.

Dr Harold agreed to join us (what a surprise!) if we really needed him.

8. Quotation mark

a. Use quotation marks to set off a direct quotation- a person's exact words.

Direct quotation – Akhila said, "I am going to college"

b. Use quotation marks for titles of short stories, poems, essays, articles, chapters and other parts of books and periodicals.

"Stopping by Woods in a Snowy Evening" is my favourite poem by Robert Frost.

c. Use a quotation mark to enclose technical terms and other words that are used in an unusual or ironic way.

He is graduating in Aviation, but he has a 'fear of heights

d. Use quotation marks to indicate quotations from another writer.

As Paulo Coelho puts it, "it's the possibility of having a dream come true that makes life interesting."

9. **Hyphen**

a. Use a hyphen to divide a word at the end of a line.

If we need to break-word, divide only on syllable breaks. Never divide one-syllable words. When you divide a word of more than one syllable, divide it between its syllables.

b. Hyphenate is a compound adjective that appears before a noun.

This is a world-famous monument.
She likes to wear brightly- coloured ornaments.
Note: Do not use a hyphen when the words appear after the form of the verb, "to be" unless the dictionary indicates so.
This monument is world-famous.

10. **Dashes**

The common types of dashes are em dash [?] and en dash [-]
<u>Em dash</u>
Use and em dash :

1. To mark off ideas that are not essential to the understanding of the rest of the sentence but too important to enclose in parentheses.

   My new student ? one who came from Indo-American high school? is an athlete.

2. To mark an abrupt change or break in thought.

   Let me recall it ? yes ? it was on Sunday.
   <u>En dash</u>
   An en dash is shorter than an em dash and longer than a hyphen. It is used to mark ranges and with the meaning "to or through" within a range of numbers.
   Pages 125 – 150; Shakespeare (1564-1616)

11. Ellipsis point

Ellipsis points are three equally spaced periods (...) to indicate the omission of words in a quotation. They are also known as suspension points.

Siddharth told me that last Sunday he went to see ... Gladiator.

[Here the writer has omitted the words Ridly Scott's historical drama film]

12. Exclamation mark

It is used after interjections and at the end of statements when a strong emotion is being expressed.
"Wow! You are selected for the team."
"How dare you speak like this!"
"Alas! Daisy is ill"

13. Question mark

A question mark is used at the end of a sentence or phrase to indicate a direct question.
Who is your captain?
Where are you going?

14. Slash

1. The slash is used to indicate the word 'or.'

   Dear Sir / Madam.

2. Use a slash to indicate 'per' in measurements of speed, prices etc.

   Petrol cost ?100/litre.
   The speed limit is 45 km/h.

3. A slash is used in dates to separate day month and year.

   28/10/1982.

4. Slash is used for certain abbreviations.

   c/o care of.
   a/c account.
   w/o without

Bibliography

- Martin & Wren. *High School English Grammar and Composition*. New Delhi:S.Chand,2001.
- Warriner, John E. Francis Griffith. *English Grammar and Composition*. The U.S.A: Harcourt Brace Jovanovich, 1977.